A Visit to

MALAYSIA

by Charis Mather

Minneapolis, Minnesota

Credits

All images are courtesy of Shutterstock.com, unless otherwise specified. With thanks to Getty Images, Thinkstock Photo, and iStockphoto.

Cover – JeremyRichards, Dudarev Mikhail. 2–3 – Sean Pavone. 4–5 – Alen thien, Matis75. 6–7 – Julinzy, ESB Professional. 8–9 – Migel, FiledIMAGE. 10–11 – michel arnault, Juhku. 12–13 – Christian Reinwald, corlaffra. 14–15 – ahau1969, Darren Kurnia. 16–17 – Katesalin Heinio, Yatra. 18–19 – Dolly MJ, NAUFAL ZAQUAN, 20–21 – msyaraafiq, CHEN WS. 22–23 – alifsufri, PaulWong.

Library of Congress Cataloging-in-Publication Data is available at www.loc.gov or upon request from the publisher.

ISBN: 979-8-88509-042-1 (hardcover)
ISBN: 979-8-88509-053-7 (paperback)
ISBN: 979-8-88509-064-3 (ebook)

© 2023 Booklife Publishing
This edition is published by arrangement with Booklife Publishing.

North American adaptations © 2023 Bearport Publishing Company. All rights reserved. No part of this publication may be reproduced in whole or in part, stored in any retrieval system, or transmitted in any form or by any means, electronic, mechanical, photocopying, recording, or otherwise, without written permission from the publisher.

For more information, write to Bearport Publishing, 5357 Penn Avenue South, Minneapolis, MN 55419. Printed in the United States of America.

CONTENTS

Country to Country 4
Today's Trip Is to Malaysia! 6
Kuala Lumpur 8
Gunung Mulu 10
Deer Cave 12
Rain Forests 14
Animals 16
Food and Drinks 18
Festivals 20
Before You Go 22
Glossary 24
Index 24

COUNTRY TO COUNTRY

A country is an area of land marked by **borders**. The people in each country have their own rules and ways of living. They may speak different languages.

Which country do you live in?

Each country around the world has its own interesting things to see and do. Let's take a trip to visit a country and learn more!

Have you ever visited another country?

TODAY'S TRIP IS TO
MALAYSIA!

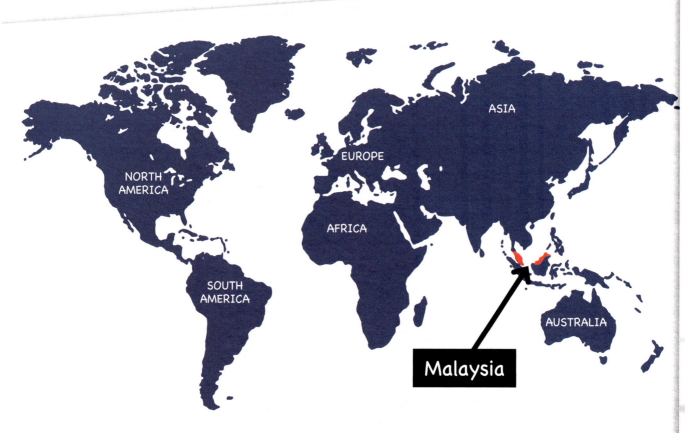

Malaysia is a country in the **continent** of Asia.

FACT FILE

Capital city:
Kuala Lumpur
Main language:
Malay
Currency: Ringgit
Flag:

Currency is the type of money that is used in a country.

7

KUALA LUMPUR

We'll start our trip in Kuala Lumpur, the capital city of Malaysia. This modern city has many tall buildings, including two twin towers. The towers are more than 1,475 feet (450 m) tall.

We can also go to the Central Market. This shopping area in Kuala Lumpur has been around for many years. Lots of people sell handmade **crafts** at the market.

Central Market

GUNUNG MULU

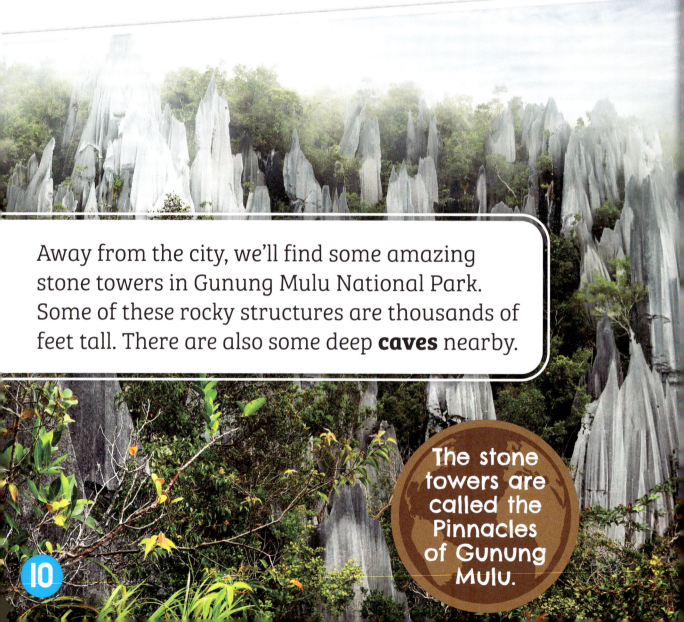

Away from the city, we'll find some amazing stone towers in Gunung Mulu National Park. Some of these rocky structures are thousands of feet tall. There are also some deep **caves** nearby.

The stone towers are called the Pinnacles of Gunung Mulu.

Visitors use walking paths with ladders to get to the stone towers. People are not allowed to build roads in Gunung Mulu so that the park stays protected.

DEER CAVE

One part of Gunung Mulu National Park has a huge cave called Deer Cave. Inside, it is about 560 ft (170 m) tall and more than 6,560 ft (2,000 m) long.

This cave is deep and dark. But lots of plants and animals live near the entrance where sunlight reaches. Millions of bats fly out of Deer Cave every evening to look for food.

The bats fly together in cloud-like shapes.

RAIN FORESTS

Malaysia is covered in **rain forests**. Thousands of plants grow in these beautiful places. There are so many trees that it is difficult for sunlight to reach the forest floor.

A Rafflesia flower can grow bigger than 3 ft (1 m) wide.

One plant in the Malaysian rain forests is very different from the rest. The Rafflesia plant has the largest flower in the world. The flower has a terrible smell like rotten meat!

ANIMALS

Many animals live in the Malaysian rain forests, including orangutans. These apes have long arms and orange fur.

Orangutans can use their feet just like their hands.

Malaysia is also home to the world's smallest bear, called the sun bear. This bear has long claws, which help it climb trees and find food. The light-colored mark on its chest gives the sun bear its name.

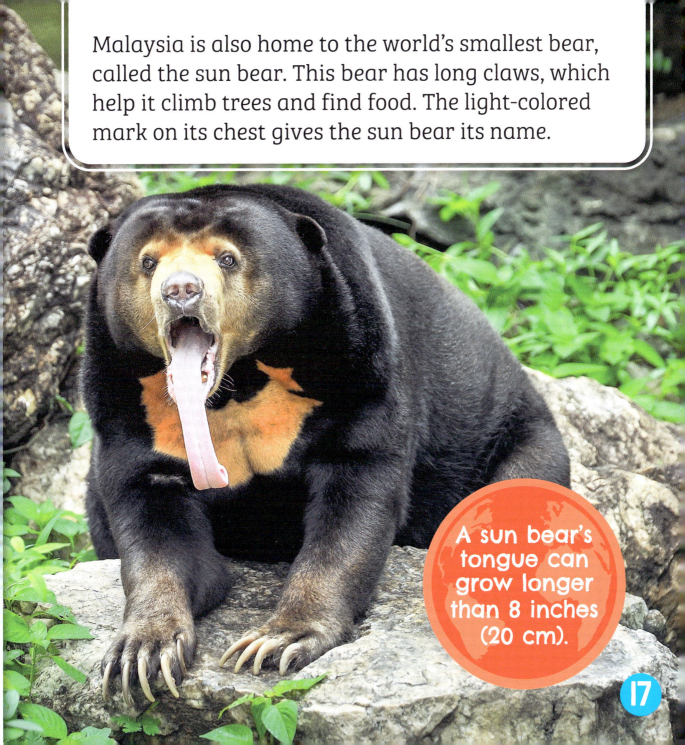

A sun bear's tongue can grow longer than 8 inches (20 cm).

FOOD AND DRINKS

Let's grab something to eat! One of the most common meals in Malaysia is nasi lemak. This dish includes coconut milk, rice, cucumber, peanuts, fried fish, and a spicy sauce. Sometimes, it is served on a leaf.

Nasi lemak

Teh tarik is a sweet, milky tea that is popular in Malaysia. It has **foam** on top that is made by pouring the tea from one glass to another.

FESTIVALS

Next, it's time to celebrate! Many different groups of people live in Malaysia. Each group has its own **festivals** to share. This means people in Malaysia might have celebrations every month!

In one part of Malaysia, people gather to celebrate Gawai Dayak. This festival includes lots of food and activities. Some people wear **traditional** clothes.

BEFORE YOU GO

Stairs leading to the Batu Caves

We can't forget to see the Batu Caves! The colorful stairs leading up to the caves are very popular. People also visit this area to see the **shrines** and to go rock climbing.

Finally, let's visit Mount Kinabalu. After a difficult walk to the top, we'll have a view from the highest place in Malaysia. It is more than 13,120 ft (4,000 m) tall.

Mount Kinabalu

What have you learned about Malaysia on this trip?

GLOSSARY

borders lines that show where one place ends and another begins

caves large openings underground or in rocks and hills

continent one of the world's seven large land masses

crafts things that take skill to make by hand

festivals events for lots of people to come together and celebrate

foam a frothy liquid with lots of small air bubbles

rain forests forests that are very hot and get a lot of rainfall

shrines places that are built to honor and remember an event or being

traditional relating to something that a group of people have done for many years

INDEX

bats 13
caves 10, 12–13, 22
food 13, 15, 17–18, 21
orangutans 16
plants 13–15
stone towers 10–11
sun bears 17
tea 19